PRESIDENTIAL MISADVENTURES

POEMS THAT POKE FUN AT THE MAN IN CHARGE

by BOB RACZKA

art by DAN E. BURR

RIGHT TURN

LEFT TURN

YIELD

GETTYSBURG ADDRESS

ROARING BROOK PRESS
NEW YORK

ALSO BY **BOB RACZKA**

Lemonade: and Other Poems Squeezed from a Single Word

Text copyright © 2015 by Bob Raczka
Illustrations copyright © 2015 by Dan E. Burr
Published by Roaring Brook Press
Roaring Brook Press is a division of Holtzbrinck Publishing Holdings
Limited Partnership
175 Fifth Avenue, New York, New York 10010
mackids.com
All rights reserved

Library of Congress Cataloging-in-Publication Data

Raczka, Bob, author.
    Presidential misadventures : poems that poke fun at the man in charge / Bob Raczka ;
illustrated by Dan E. Burr. – First edition.
        pages cm
    Summary: "A book of poetry about the presidents written in clerihews"–Provided by
publisher.
    ISBN 978-1-59643-980-1 (hardback) – ISBN 978-1-59643-981-8 (ebook)
    1. Presidents–United States–Juvenile poetry. 2. Children's poetry, American. I. Title.
    PS3618.A346P74 2015
    811'.6–dc23

                                                                                    2014032639

Roaring Brook Press books may be purchased for business or promotional use. For
information on bulk purchases please contact Macmillan Corporate and Premium Sales
Department at (800) 221-7945 x5442 or by email at specialmarkets@macmillan.com.

First edition 2015
Book design by Andrew Arnold
Printed in the United States of America by Worzalla, Steven's Point, Wisonsin

1 3 5 7 9 10 8 6 4 2

CONTENTS

George Washington ... 1

John Adams 2

Thomas Jefferson 3

James Madison 4

James Monroe 4

John Quincy Adams .. 5

Andrew Jackson 6

Martin Van Buren 7

William H. Harrison .. 8

John Tyler 8

James K. Polk 9

Zachary Taylor 10

Millard Fillmore 11

Franklin Pierce 12

James Buchanan 13

Abraham Lincoln 14

Andrew Johnson 15

Ulysses S. Grant 16

Rutherford B. Hayes ...17

James Garfield 18

Chester A. Arthur 18

Grover Cleveland 19

Benjamin Harrison 20

William McKinley 21

Theodore Roosevelt 22

William Howard Taft ...23

Woodrow Wilson 24

Warren G. Harding 25

Calvin Coolidge 26

Herbert Hoover. 27

Franklin D. Roosevelt 28

Harry S. Truman 29

Dwight D. Eisenhower 30

John F. Kennedy 31

Lyndon B. Johnson 32

Richard M. Nixon 33

Gerald R. Ford 34

James Carter 34

Ronald Reagan 35

George H. W. Bush 36

William J. Clinton 37

George W. Bush 38

Barack Obama 39

Appendix 40

IN **1890,** a fifteen-year-old English schoolboy named Edmund Clerihew Bentley was sitting in science class learning about the famous English scientist Sir Humphry Davy. To amuse himself, Edmund wrote a little poem in his notebook poking fun at Sir Humphry:

> *Sir Humphry Davy*
> *Abominated gravy.*
> *He lived in the odium*
> *Of having discovered sodium.*

Edmund showed the poem to his classmates, who laughed and started writing their own. And that's how the "clerihew" was born. Eventually, Edmund published several collections of these poems and they became quite popular.

Clerihews are fun to write because they have just a few simple rules:

- The clerihew is a four-line poem that pokes fun at a famous person
- The first two lines rhyme, and the last two lines rhyme (AABB)
- The first line contains (and usually ends with) the name of the famous person
- The meter is irregular; in other words, each line can have a different number of beats

Here's another example, which I wrote about Henry Ford:

> *Model T man Henry Ford*
> *Made a car folks could afford.*
> *But it only came in black.*
> *Want a red car? Sorry, Jack.*

As you can see, the first line ends with a famous name (Henry Ford); the poem pokes fun at Henry (he made a car that only came in one color); the first two lines rhyme (Ford, afford); and the last two lines rhyme (black, Jack).

I didn't follow the last rule, which says the meter should be irregular, because I like to write in a regular meter. But I still think the poem is funny, so it works for me. You can bend the rules too. The important thing is to have fun.

For this book, I decided to make fun of some guys who are seriously famous—and famously serious: the presidents of the United States. I hope you find them both historical and hysterical!

—BOB

Toothache-prone **GEORGE WASHINGTON**
complained that flossing was no fun.
Lifelong dental misadventures
led to presidential dentures.

Ambitious bachelor **JOHN ADAMS**
promised Abigail, "Madam,
if you choose to be my spouse,
we'll live in a big white house."

Spendthrift **THOMAS JEFFERSON**
declared, "My shopping's never done."
He went to town to buy bananas
and came home with Louisiana.

Founding dad **JAMES MADISON**
was sad he never had a son.
His parental contribution?
Father of the Constitution.

Turf defender **JAMES MONROE**
warned the Europeans, "Whoa!
If you trespass, you'll be shot.
That's my doctrine, like it or not."

Fitness nut **JOHN QUINCY ADAMS**
lived by the words, "Up and at 'em."
Every morning, right at dawn,
he swam the Potomac with no clothes on.

Dueling enthusiast **ANDREW JACKSON**
suffered from a bullet attraction.
Two in his arm and one in his chest–
he sure could have used a bulletproof vest.

Tiger-cub owner **MARTIN VAN BUREN**
played with his kitties without a concern.
He wanted to raise them, for he was no coward,
but Congress feared headlines like,
    "MARTIN DEVOURED."

Newly elected
WILLIAM H. HARRISON

spoke for two hours,
    defying comparison.
Soon after, he suffered
    an untimely death.
Apparently he was
    out of breath.

Family builder
JOHN TYLER

was a champion
    child stockpiler.
Fifteen sons and
    daughters in all,
more names than John
    could ever recall.

Country enlarger **JAMES K. POLK**
added one-third of our map—no joke.
He said, "It's all ours, from sea to sea,"
calling it "Manifest Destiny."

Tobacco chewer **ZACHARY TAYLOR**
was a long-range saliva air-mailer.
Ask any man in his platoon—
they say he never missed a spittoon.

Book collector **MILLARD FILLMORE**
owned a ton, but wanted still more.
Believing that books make us less barbarian,
Millard became the first White House librarian.

"Handsome Frank," or **_FRANKLIN PIERCE_**,
must have loved what he saw in mirrors.
Despite the fact that he had good looks,
you don't see him much in the history books.

Pennsylvanian **JAMES BUCHANAN**
had poor taste in party plannin'.
For dinner, he often served sauerkraut.
No doubt for dessert it was brussels sprouts.

Self-educated **ABRAHAM LINCOLN**
had a knack for original thinkin'.
To keep track of where his speeches were at,
he kept them tucked in his stovepipe hat.

Generally frugal **ANDREW JOHNSON**
never bought bratwurst or beer in Wisconsin.
He never bought corn-fed beef in Nebraska.
However, he bought all the ice in Alaska.

Expert horseman **U. S. GRANT**
loved to make his ponies pant.
His riding skills were unsurpassed,
though he once got a ticket for going too fast.

Forward-thinking **RUTHERFORD HAYES**
was quick to join the telephone craze.
To prove his importance was second to none,
Rutherford's telephone number was "1."

Ambidextrous
JAMES GARFIELD
had talents he rarely revealed.
For instance, his curious
writing technique—
one hand wrote in
Latin, the other in Greek.

Fashion-conscious
CHESTER ARTHUR
pushed the boundaries
of style farther.
He owned more than
eighty pairs of pants,
which he changed whenever
he got the chance.

Overweight candidate **GROVER CLEVELAND** decided to drop his first name, Stephen. Now he's the answer to this clever riddle: Which U.S. president led with his middle?

Electric-shock victim **BENJAMIN HARRISON**

harbored a fear that was very embarrassin'.

When he went to bed at night,

Ben was afraid to turn out the light.

Glad-hander **WILLIAM McKINLEY**
spread his goodwill rather thinly.
Meeting folks made him feel so empowered,
he shook hands with more than 2,000 per hour.

Rough Rider **THEODORE ROOSEVELT**
was shot near the heart, which he hardly felt.
The bullet was slowed by a fifty-page speech,
which Teddy still gave. That's a "tough" you
can't teach.

Three hundred pounder **WILLIAM H. TAFT**
vaguely resembled a blimplike craft.
He sat down to do the rub-a-dub-dub,
but due to his girth, he got stuck in the tub.

Avid golfer **WOODROW WILSON**
played year-round 'cause he thought it was fun.
While most guys hang up their bags in the fall,
Woodrow played in the snow with black balls.

Former newsman **WARREN G. HARDING** made the headlines upon his departing: "PRESIDENT LEAVES BIG SHOES TO FILL." His size 14 feet are a record still.

Cowboy wannabe **CALVIN COOLIDGE**
wasn't afraid of looking foolish.
He loved to ride his mechanical horse—
wearing a ten-gallon hat, of course.

Mr. and Mrs. **HERBERT HOOVER**
were known as eavesdropping disapprovers.
To keep folks from listening to what they said,
they spoke not in English but Chinese instead.

Hat fan **FRANKLIN D. ROOSEVELT**
wore a fedora made of felt.
The president felt it made him dashing,
but Eleanor felt it needed trashing.

Nearsighted **HARRY S. TRUMAN**
loved reading like no other human.
When he discovered that knowledge is free,
he read every book in the library.

Gourmet **DWIGHT D. EISENHOWER**

flavored his soup with nasturtium flowers.

Ike loved to cook, and here's more proof:

He often grilled steaks on the White House roof.

Cold War president **JFK**
smoked four to five cigars a day.
Cuban stogies topped his list,
despite being rolled by Communists.

Fresca fanatic **LBJ**
wanted his pop without delay.
Free refills at the push of a button
turned Lyndon into a soda glutton.

Cover-upper **RICHARD NIXON**
told a lie he couldn't fix. Instead of waiting to be impeached,
he gave the first resignation speech.

Football player
GERALD FORD
had tackling skills the
    pros adored.
He could have played for
    Detroit if he liked,
but Jerry decided to
    fight tax hikes.

Energy-conscious
JIMMY CARTER
set an example by
    dressing smarter.
To save on heat he wore
    cardigan sweaters.
Unfortunately, he was
    not a trendsetter.

Jelly-bean lover **RONALD REAGAN** reached for these sweets again and again. Perhaps the long life of "Mr. Conservative" was due to this candy's preservatives.

Dog owner **GEORGE H. W. BUSH**
trained Millie, his spaniel, to sit on her tush.
As dog tricks go, this one isn't stellar,
but she did write a *New York Times* bestseller.

Casual jogger **_BILL CLINTON_**
was not interested in sprintin'—
unless he had cravings for meat on a bun.
Then he would go on a fast-food run.

Relaxer-in-chief **GEORGE W. BUSH** discovered the nation's top job was cush. He took more than 900 days of vacation, a record for two-term administrations.

White House hopeful **BARACK OBAMA**
gave a speech astride a llama.
"You can't do that," critics panned.
He responded, "Yes we can."

APPENDIX

1. GEORGE WASHINGTON Of course, Washington lived long before dental floss was invented. And despite popular belief, he never had wooden teeth. However, Washington did wear dentures made from gold, ivory, and lead—not to mention human teeth and horse teeth.

2. JOHN ADAMS John and Abigail Adams were the first presidential couple to live in the White House. They moved in before it was completed—or white. The gray sandstone house was painted white after being burned by the British in 1814.

3. THOMAS JEFFERSON Jefferson was a big spender and left the White House in debt. But he got a good deal when he bought the Louisiana Territory from France for $15 million (3 cents an acre). At the time, this nearly doubled the size of the country.

4. JAMES MADISON Madison had no sons or daughters of his own, but he did become a stepfather when he married Dolley. She was a widow with a son named John. Madison not only championed our constitution, but also authored its first ten amendments—the Bill of Rights.

5. JAMES MONROE In an 1823 speech, Monroe warned Europe not to interfere in the affairs of the Western Hemisphere, including all of North and South America. He said any interference would be treated as an act of aggression, and the United States would retaliate.

6. JOHN QUINCY ADAMS To get exercise during his presidency, Adams walked more than three miles a day. He also loved to swim naked in the Potomac River. He preferred to swim early in the morning, getting up at 5:00 a.m. and 4:15 a.m. in the summer.

7. ANDREW JACKSON In a duel against Charles Dickinson, Jackson let Dickinson shoot first. He shot Jackson in the chest. The bullet broke two of Jackson's ribs and lodged inches from his heart, but didn't kill him. Jackson then shot and killed Dickinson.

8. MARTIN VAN BUREN Van Buren received two tiger cubs as a gift from the Sultan of Oman—an Arab state. He enjoyed showing them off to White House visitors, but Congress said they belonged to the American people. So he donated them to the National Zoo.

9. WILLIAM HENRY HARRISON At his inauguration, Harrison spoke for nearly two hours. His speech was 8,445 words long, the longest in presidential history. One month later he died of pneumonia, which may have been caused by his long exposure to cold, wet weather on Inauguration Day.

10. JOHN TYLER Tyler had eight children with his first wife, Letitia, who died in the White House. After he remarried, he had seven children with his second wife, Julia. Of his fifteen children, the most by any U.S. president, seven were boys and eight were girls.

11. JAMES K. POLK During Polk's presidency, the United States added more land than

Jefferson's Louisiana Purchase. After annexing Texas and taking over Oregon from Great Britain, Polk went to war with Mexico and acquired what later became Arizona, New Mexico, Nevada, Utah, and California.

12. ZACHARY TAYLOR   Taylor spent forty years of his life in the military and was a career officer. He did not smoke, but like many men of his time, he chewed tobacco. Taylor claimed he could hit the spittoons in the White House from a distance of twelve feet.

13. MILLARD FILLMORE   Fillmore and his wife, Abigail, were both book lovers. Together, they created a collection of about 200 books that they left to the nation—the first White House library. Fillmore's personal collection included some 4,000 volumes.

14. FRANKLIN PIERCE   According to one historian, Pierce was "arguably the most handsome man ever to serve as president of the United States." However, most rank him among the worst presidents in our history. After his first term, his own party refused to renominate him.

15. JAMES BUCHANAN   Before he became president, Buchanan often hosted sauerkraut and mashed potato parties at his home in Pennsylvania. According to Buchanan, no one made better sauerkraut than his housekeeper, "Miss Hetty" Parker.

16. ABRAHAM LINCOLN   When Lincoln was a lawyer, his office was a mess, so he often used his hat to carry notes, letters, bills, and even speeches. According to one story, a group of mischievous boys once rigged up a wire to knock his hat off, and papers flew everywhere.

17. ANDREW JOHNSON   In 1867, Johnson agreed to buy the Alaskan territory from Russia for $7.2 million. People laughed at the idea, calling it Johnson's "polar bear garden." But in a few years gold was discovered there, and later, oil. Alaska didn't become a state until 1959.

18. ULYSSES S. GRANT   Grant often raced through the streets of Washington on horseback or in a horse-drawn carriage. Once he was stopped by a policeman, who was embarrassed when he found out he had pulled over the president. But Grant insisted on paying the fine.

19. RUTHERFORD B. HAYES   After talking to Alexander Graham Bell on his recent invention, the telephone, Hayes decided to have one installed in the White House. He called it "one of the greatest events since creation." But he rarely used it, since few people had phones at the time.

20. JAMES GARFIELD   Although he was primarily left-handed, Garfield could write with both hands. Even more impressive, if you asked him a question in English, he could write the answer in two different languages at the same time—with one hand in Latin and the other in Greek.

21. CHESTER A. ARTHUR   Nicknamed "Elegant Arthur," this president was known for his outlandish sideburns, his lavish parties, and his expensive refurbishing of the White House. Those who knew him said he owned eighty pairs of pants, which he changed several times a day.

22. & 24. GROVER CLEVELAND Stephen Grover Cleveland weighed more than 250 pounds, so friends started calling him "Big Steve"—a nickname he probably disliked. At any rate, he dropped "Stephen." Two other presidents also dropped their first names—John Calvin Coolidge and Thomas Woodrow Wilson.

23. BENJAMIN HARRISON Harrison hired the Edison General Electric Company to install electric lights in the White House. But after he received a shock from a light switch, he and his wife were afraid of being electrocuted and often went to bed with the lights on.

25. WILLIAM McKINLEY McKinley never seemed to get tired of shaking hands. He even had his own technique, which people called the "McKinley grip." During one public reception in 1900, he shook hands with 4,816 people in one hour and forty-five minutes. That's more than forty-five handshakes per minute.

26. THEODORE ROOSEVELT In 1912, just before a speech in Milwaukee, Roosevelt was shot in the chest by a man named John Schrank. Thanks to the fifty-page speech and glasses case in his breast pocket, the bullet did not reach his heart. He spoke for ninety minutes—and the bullet was never removed.

27. WILLIAM HOWARD TAFT At nearly six feet tall and 340 pounds, Taft is the most obese president we've ever had. Legend has it that when he got stuck in the White House bathtub, it took six aides to pull him out—and the replacement tub was big enough to hold four men.

28. WOODROW WILSON Wilson played more than 1,000 rounds of golf during his time in office, which is a presidential record. In the winter, the Secret Service painted Wilson's golf balls black so he could play in the snow on the White House lawn.

29. WARREN G. HARDING Harding spent more than thirty years as the publisher of a newspaper, the *Marion Daily Star*, which he bought with partners when he was just nineteen years old. He also wore size 14 shoes, making his feet the biggest of all the presidents.

30. CALVIN COOLIDGE Coolidge once received a mechanical horse as a gag gift. He stuck it in a dressing room, with no intention of using it, but someone dared him to try it. He ended up loving it, always wearing a cowboy hat when he rode. Ironically, he was allergic to horses.

31. HERBERT HOOVER Before he was president, Hoover was a mining engineer in China. While he was there, Hoover and his wife learned to speak Mandarin Chinese. Later, in the White House, they spoke Chinese to each other when they wanted to prevent eavesdropping.

32. FRANKLIN D. ROOSEVELT   FDR often wore hats on the campaign trail and considered some of them lucky. For some reason, Mrs. Roosevelt did not like one particular gray felt hat. To keep Franklin from wearing it, she gave it to his valet as a gift.

33. HARRY S. TRUMAN   Because he wore glasses at a young age, Truman steered clear of boyhood activities that might break them. He became a voracious reader instead. It's commonly believed that he read all 3,000 books in the Independence, Missouri, library before he was fifteen.

34. DWIGHT D. EISENHOWER   Eisenhower really did enjoy cooking. One of his favorite recipes was for vegetable soup. His "secret" ingredient was nasturtium stems. He also loved grilling salt-encrusted steaks on the White House roof—directly on the hot coals.

35. JOHN F. KENNEDY   In 1962, Kennedy asked one of his aides to buy him 1,200 Cuban cigars. Once they were purchased, Kennedy signed a trade embargo with Communist Cuba, which made the purchase of any products made in Cuba illegal—including cigars.

36. LYNDON B. JOHNSON   When he became president, Johnson quit drinking alcohol. He drank coffee, tea, Coke, and Fresca instead. But Fresca, a grapefruit-flavored drink, was his favorite. By pushing a button in the Oval Office, he could have one whenever he liked.

37. RICHARD M. NIXON   Nixon was the first president to visit Communist China. But he is best remembered for being the only president to resign. He was held responsible when people who worked for him stole documents from the Watergate Hotel in Washington, D.C., and he lied about it.

38. GERALD R. FORD   During his college career at the University of Michigan, Ford played center and linebacker. His teams were undefeated in 1932 and 1933, and he was voted MVP in 1934. He turned down offers to play for both the Detroit Lions and the Green Bay Packers.

39. JAMES CARTER   During his presidency, Carter encouraged Americans to conserve energy. He had solar panels put on the White House, turned down the heat, and wore cardigan sweaters. He even wore one when he appeared on TV to talk about the energy crisis.

40. RONALD REAGAN   Reagan started eating jelly beans to help him quit smoking. His favorite brand was Jelly Belly. In fact, the company sent three and a half tons of red, white, and blue jelly beans to the White House for his inauguration. His favorite flavor was licorice.

41. GEORGE H. W. BUSH   George and Barbara Bush had a pet springer spaniel named Millie, who is listed as the author of *Millie's Book: As Dictated to Barbara Bush*. It became a *New York Times* bestseller, with proceeds going to the Barbara Bush Foundation for Family Literacy.

42. WILLIAM J. CLINTON While in office, Clinton was an avid jogger, running about three times a week. But he was also known for his love of fast food. This eventually caught up with him, when he had quadruple bypass surgery in 2004. His arteries were more than ninety percent blocked.

43. GEORGE W. BUSH During eight years as president, Bush spent all or part of 477 days at Camp David, the presidential retreat in Maryland. He also made seventy-seven trips to his Texas ranch, where he spent all or part of 490 days. That's 967 days—or thirty-two percent of his time in office—on vacation.

44. BARACK OBAMA Obama became the first U.S. president of African American descent. His slogan during the 2008 presidential campaign was "Yes we can." It came from the Spanish phrase, "*Si se puede*," the motto of the United Farm Workers union.

GENERAL REFERENCE

WEB SITES

American Presidents Blog: american-presidents.org
History Channel: history.com/this-day-in-history
Library of Congress, the Wise Guide: loc.gov/wiseguide
Presidents of the United States Web site: potus.com
Prologue Magazine, National Archives: archives.gov/publications/prologue
White House Web site: whitehouse.gov/about/presidents

BOOKS

Beyer, Rick. *The Greatest Presidential Stories Never Told: 100 Tales from History to Astonish, Bewilder, and Stupefy.* Harper. 2007.

Davis, Kenneth C. *Don't Know Much About the American Presidents.* Hyperion. 2012.

Davis, Todd, and Marc Fey. *The New Big Book of U.S. Presidents: Fascinating Facts About Each and Every President, Including an American History Timeline.* Running Press Kids. 2009.

DeGragario, William. *The Complete Book of U.S. Presidents: From George Washington to George W. Bush.* Gramercy. 1997.

Matuz, Roger. *The Presidents Fact Book: A Comprehensive Handbook to the Achievements, Events, People, Triumphs, and Tragedies of Every President from George Washington to George W. Bush.* Black Dog & Leventhal Publishers. 2004.

Sullivan, George. *Facts and Fun About the Presidents.* Scholastic Paperbacks. 1994.